American Archaeology
UNCOVERS
THE DUTCH COLONIES

LOIS MINER HUEY

 Marshall Cavendish
Benchmark
New York

ACKNOWLEDGMENTS

Consultant: James W. Bradley,
Director, Robert S. Peabody
Museum of Archaeology at Phillips Academy

Marshall Cavendish • 99 White Plains Road • Tarrytown, New York 10591
www.marshallcavendish.us

Library of Congress Cataloging–in–Publication Data

Huey, Lois Miner.
American archeology uncovers the Dutch colonies / by Lois Miner Huey.
p. cm. — (American archaeology)
Includes bibliographical references and index.
ISBN 978–0–7614–4263–9
1. New Netherland—History—Juvenile literature.
2. NewNetherland—Antiquities—Juvenile literature.
3. Archaeology andhistory—Juvenile literature.
4. Dutch—North America—History—Juvenileliterature.
5. Netherlands—Colonies—America—Juvenile literature. I. Title.
F122.1.H798 2010
974.7'102—dc22
2008050187

Photo research by: Tracey Engel

Cover photo, top: Students conduct a dig at a university's science camp.
Artifacts at bottom: left, a dish fragment found in a New Amsterdam warehouse; center, a coin used by Dutch
colonists; right, a stem from a spigot, found at a Dutch farm.

Cover photo: AP Images/Bob Child (top); Printed with permission of the New York State Museum, Albany,
NY, 12230 (bottom, left); Shutterstock/Jens Stolt (bottom, center); From the Collection of Bobby Brustle,
photographed by Joseph McEvoy (bottom, right) iStock © Lisa Thorinberg, iStock © Vishnu Mulakala, back
cover; iStock © Alex Nikado
The photographs in this book are used by permission and through the courtesy of: Alamy: The Print Collector,
20 (bottom); North Wind Picture Archives, 26 (bottom), 54–55; Peter Casolino, 42–43; Reinhard Dirscherl,
48–49. Albany Institute of History and Art: Fireback, unidentified marker, The Netherlands, 1665, Cast iron,
Gift of Mrs. Richard P. Schuyler, 31. AP Images: Bob Child, 4 (bottom); Mitch Jacobson, 10. The Bridgeman
Art Library International: Ashmolean Museum, University of Oxford, UK, 21 (bottom). Getty Images: National
Geographic/Joseph H. Bailey, 50; The Bridgeman Art Library/Pieter de Hooch, 56. The Granger Collection, New
York: 37 (bottom). Institute of Nautical Archaeology: 52. From the Collection of Bobby Brustle, photographed
by Joseph McEvoy: 32 (both). Printed with permission of the New York State Museum, Albany, NY, 12230:
5 (bottom), 17 (top); Courtesy of First Church in Albany (Reformed), 24; 38 (both), 40, 41. New York State
Parks, Recreation and Historic Preservation: 15; Paul Huey, 17 (bottom), 33. Peabody Museum, Harvard
University, Cambridge: catalog no. 34026, 46 (all). Penn Museum object 9186, image #142826: 44. The Public
Archaeology Laboratory, Inc.: 36. Larry C. Sanders: 51. L. F. Tantillo: 12–13, 22–23, 28–29, 34–35. 3; iStock ©
Eric Isselee, 4; iStock © ObservePhoto, 5; Shutterstock © Najin, 6; iStock © Richard Goerg, iStock © Richard
Cano, 10; Shutterstock © Biuliq, 21; Shutterstock © Norman Chan
Printed in Malaysia
135642

CONTENTS

WHAT IS Historical Archaeology?

Archaeologists dig into the ground to find food bones, building remains, and tools used by people in the past. Historical archaeologists are looking for clues about what happened in America after Europeans arrived.

A group of students at the "Kids Are Scientists, Too" camp conduct an archaeological investigation at the former site of an eighteenth-century home on the University of Connecticut campus at Storrs.

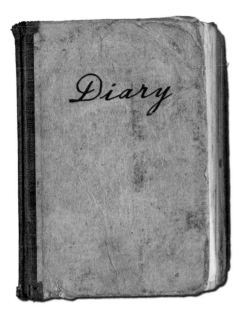

Yes, written documents tell some of the story. Historical archaeologists research documents like maps, diaries, land deeds, and letters to help understand what happened on a site. But those documents do not usually talk about regular people, the ones who did not write letters or diaries. Historical archaeologists are especially interested in learning about the lives of servants, poor farmers, and soldiers who built America.

How do archaeologists do this? By studying people's garbage.

What folks used and threw away tells more about their daily lives than objects kept on shelves out of harm's way. Archaeologists want to study the stuff that did not make it into museums—objects that were broken and discarded after much use. The garbage.

Broken dishes and glassware tell archaeologists what people of the past chose for setting their tables. Studying the bones from people's food, as well as their butchering techniques, provides information about what people ate and how they cooked. When archaeologists measure uncovered house and barn foundations, they find out how people crafted buildings, what size and shape those buildings were, and how they were used. Buttons, straight pins, gun parts, and toys are clues to how people dressed, defended their homes, and spent their leisure time.

How do historical archaeologists know they are collecting information about people who lived in the 1600s rather than people from the 1800s? They use a method called stratigraphy (struh-TIG-ra-fee). Over time, layers of soil called strata build up on a site through natural causes or when people add their own materials. By carefully scraping away the soil with small tools, archaeologists dig down through time. They begin with upper levels of soil, in which they may find nineteenth-century layers. As they work their way down, they reach eighteenth-century layers, seventeenth-century layers, and so on. In some areas, the layers go back as far as Viking times. Prehistoric Native American layers are often found at the deepest level. The scientists dig each layer separately and collect its artifacts. Once the uppermost layer has been removed, the archaeologists have dug through the lives of everyone who lived on that site at a given time.

Based on what they find, archaeologists interpret the artifacts from each time period to understand how people's lives changed. *Change* is a big word in archaeology. How people lived—and how and when that changed—is an important part of the interpretation. As new evidence appears, archaeologists sometimes have to change their interpretations. That makes archaeology really interesting.

Stratigraphy is the key to understanding the past. Sticking a shovel straight down into the ground and pulling up the soil would disturb the stratigraphy, mix up the layers, and mix up the time periods. Archaeologists use shovel testing only to find a site. Then they switch over to small tools and painstakingly remove the layers one by one.

As archaeologists study a site, they carefully draw, map, and photograph building remains. Artifacts are taken back to the lab, where workers wash and store them. Codes are written on each object so that it is clear exactly where the artifact was found. Scientists run tests on charcoal, soil, and remains found inside bottles. Then the archaeologist writes up the results of the research so everyone can know what was learned. Museum displays often follow.

The world that we think of as ours was thought by people in the past to be theirs. Our knowledge of everyday events in the lives of people who lived long ago seems to be washed away by time. By digging in the ground and studying documents, an archaeologist takes a voyage to the distant past as if he or she were in a magical time machine.

Read about archaeology in books and magazines, go to museums, watch programs on television, and maybe visit a local archaeology dig. Someday you, too, might decide to use the tools of archaeology to study the past.

The Dutch In America

Did you know that the Dutch established a colony in North America? It was called New Netherland. It stretched from today's New York State east into Connecticut and down the coast to include New Jersey, parts of Pennsylvania, and Delaware. In Europe, the Dutch live in a country that people often called Holland, after its most populated province (state). In the 1600s the country was named the United Provinces of the Netherlands. Today the official name is Kingdom of the Netherlands, but most people call it the Netherlands.

This map shows locations of The Netherlands in Europe and New Netherland along the coast of North America.

Today the Dutch are known for their wooden shoes, windmills, tulips, and cheese. In the 1600s, however, they were a leading world power. Dutch explorers sailed their ships all over the world to establish trade and colonies.

Four hundred years ago, in 1609, Holland sent an Englishman named Henry Hudson to the New World. He claimed part of today's New York State for the Dutch. This was just two years after the English settled Jamestown, Virginia, and eleven years before the Pilgrims arrived in Plymouth, Massachusetts.

By 1614, the Dutch had established a trading post far up the Hudson River near today's city of Albany, New York. In 1624 they built a permanent post nearby and called it Fort Orange. They also established trading posts or forts in New Amsterdam (today's New York City), New Jersey, Pennsylvania, Connecticut, and Delaware. Settlers came from Europe to trade and to farm.

The Half Moon

Explorer Henry Hudson sailed for the Dutch in a ship called the *Half Moon*. Researchers built a reproduction of the ship in Albany. Today, the *Half Moon* sails the Hudson River between Albany and New York City during good weather. It carries school groups, scout troops, and other modern-day explorers. Passengers help sail the ship, learn the geography of the river, and experience the lives of seventeenth-century sailors.

At home the Dutch were enjoying their Golden Age. Thanks to their success in business around the world, money poured into the country. People spent their money to build fine houses, to furnish them with rich fabrics and silver, and to have artists such as Rembrandt and Vermeer decorate their homes and government buildings.

By 1664 the English had established many colonies in North America. They decided to take New Netherland, too. The Dutch governor, a wooden-legged soldier named Peter Stuyvesant, was furious when the Dutch settlers gave in to the English rather than fighting for their land. Fort Orange and the nearby town of Beverwyck (BAY-fer-vik) became Albany. New Amsterdam became New York City. Forts in Delaware became New Castle and Wilmington.

Historians have had a tough time studying the Dutch in America. First, they have to learn to read

Dutch. Second, the Dutch colonists wrote in a challenging type of shorthand. Although there are now computer programs that translate Dutch records into English, archaeologists have discovered much of the information about the Dutch colonies in North America.

The following chapters provide a sample of some Dutch archaeological sites in North America. These sites include forts, a town, a large farm, a windmill, a warehouse, a town house, a governor's house, and even a mysterious shipwreck. Let's dig the Dutch!

This map shows locations of Dutch Fort Orange near today's Albany, New York and Dutch New Amsterdam, today's New York City.

One
A Dutch Fort

Dutch colonists built two forts near Albany, the current capital city of New York State. One, called Fort Nassau, was located on an island. This site later became covered with warehouses and oil tanks, so the fort's remains were never found. However, archaeologists discovered that Native Americans regularly went to this fort to trade.

A modern artist's interpretation of Fort Nassau, the earliest Dutch fort near Albany. The fort and trading post were built very near where Henry Hudson's ship anchored in 1609.

Excavations on the riverbank directly across from Fort Nassau revealed a Native American encampment. Trash pits yielded Indian artifacts such as wampum and stone tools mixed with Dutch objects such as yellow bricks, white clay pipes, blue and white tiles, glassware, and a small musical instrument called a mouth harp.

The location of the other fort, Fort Orange, eventually disappeared from memory—until it was almost lost forever.

To the Rescue

In the 1960s construction began on Interstate Highway 787, a north-south expressway that runs along the Hudson River, passing between Albany and the river. One historical archaeologist became convinced that the site of Fort Orange lay buried in the highway's path. Local experts disagreed. As it turned out, they had not done proper map research. The archaeologist had overlaid an entire series of maps, beginning with the earliest (1632) and ending with maps from the twentieth century. The maps clearly showed that over time, people had dumped fill that moved the shoreline of the Hudson River. The site of Fort Orange, once located right on the river, was now inland—and in the path of the rapidly approaching highway.

Finally, state officials agreed to send a machine to dig where the archaeologist thought the site was located. Imagine the excitement when the machine pulled up early Dutch artifacts including clay pipes, glass, and pottery—the first ever found in the Albany area!

That was in October 1970. It was too late to stop the highway. Cold weather was coming. The state transportation department agreed to build a shelter, Albany's mayor sent space heaters, and the archaeological crew settled down to a grueling winter of working seven days a week to rescue information that otherwise would be lost.

A view of the site of Fort Orange during winter excavations. The shelter was erected just one day before this snowstorm arrived.

Golden Oldies

The results of the Fort Orange excavations were a big surprise. Historians had assumed that the first Dutch settlers, like those in the English settlements of Jamestown and Plymouth, had had a tough time. However, in the early Dutch layers of Fort Orange, archaeologists found delicate glassware, fine ceramics, and food bones from deer, cows, pigs, and sheep. The colonists had brought with them many items that they enjoyed at home in their Golden Age.

The archaeologist also studied the fort itself. It was built with a wall made of horizontally stacked logs rather than the more common vertical ones. A stone-lined moat helped protect it from Native American attacks (which never came). Inside the gate was a guardhouse with a brick foundation.

Eight wooden houses for soldiers lay along one inside wall. Other houses, built by traders, had wood-lined cellars. The houses were made of red bricks as well as small, yellow, typically Dutch bricks. The Dutch settlers built houses quickly by digging a large cellar hole and then lining the walls and floor with wood planks. To support the floors and walls above, they made columns out of wood posts standing on bricks. A house like this lasted about twenty years.

In the middle of the fort stood a large, elegant building used for administration and storage; later it was replaced by a fancy brick courthouse. The roofs of the buildings were covered with red tiles, and some of the buildings had whitewashed walls lined with blue-painted tiles, fireplaces, and fancy glass windows. The Dutch seemed to live in great comfort so far from home.

The door of the fort opened toward the river, where ships stood offshore ready to load goods for a return trip to Holland—and return with supplies for the colonists. The early Dutch colonists intended to make money through trade and return home. But many stayed. They built houses with sturdy stone foundations and settled down to a Dutch life in the New World.

One of the most exciting Fort Orange finds was a piece of window glass from a house built in 1651. Paintings of houses in the Netherlands show large windows with rectangular panes, some with a round pane in the middle. The round panes are painted with colorful designs. Several fragments of window glass excavated at Fort Orange are round and decorated with painted designs. The decoration on one appears to show a coat of arms, the name Jacob, and the date 1650. This was further evidence that the colonists enjoyed fancy houses, just like ones at home.

Food bones provided information about what the Dutch ate: mostly deer but also fish, birds such as crane and duck, cattle, sheep, bears, raccoons, and pigs. The early settlers ate what they were used to, but they also tried new foods. In Europe, deer were scarce and available only to the rich. The large quantity of deer must have been a real treat for the colonists.

Personal items included bone combs, shoe buckles, pewter spoons, and a pair of spectacles. During that time period, only scholars and the elderly wore eyeglasses. Most likely an older person lived in that house.

One comb was made from turtle shell. A woman would wear this fancy item in her hair. The type of turtle shell was from Jamaica. This means the comb must have been sent northward from the West Indies, an area where the Dutch enjoyed active trade. Other women's items included pins, thimbles, and embroidery scissors.

Archaeologists also found gun parts, as well as 3-pound (1.36-kilogram) cannon balls for cannons that sat on the fort walls. One of the cannons still exists. It is on display at the New York State Museum in Albany.

This Dutch cannon once sat on the walls of Fort Orange. The cannon was cast in Amsterdam, Holland, in 1630. It is now displayed at the New York State Museum in Albany.

Pipe stem whistles from Fort Orange.

Fun at the Fort

Life at the fort was not all work. Diggers found more than thirty broken white clay tobacco pipe stems with wedge-shaped holes carved in them. These stems worked like small flutes. When someone blew into the end of the pipe stem, a whistle-like sound was produced. Perhaps these were signaling devices or, more likely, something fun for the soldiers to do while on duty.

Mouth harps also are common on Dutch sites. At first, harps were made of iron, but they were brass by the 1640s. Mouth harps are held carefully against the teeth. The player flicks a thin metal tang with a finger, which causes it to vibrate and make a musical sound. Mouth harps were so popular that a German composer later wrote concert music for mouth harp and orchestra!

Peaceful Trade

The Dutch were used to dealing with Native peoples around the world. Their policy toward the Native Americans was "do no harm." Anywhere they settled in North America, they were careful to negotiate with local people to purchase land.

The Dutch relied on Native Americans to come to the fort with animal pelts, especially beaver, which were highly prized in Europe for making hats and other items. The Native Americans came to trade for European-made items such as scissors, brass kettles, glass beads, mirrors, and wool blankets.

The Dutch quickly learned that the Native Americans near Fort Orange especially loved shell beads called wampum. Believing that wampum had magical properties, Indians exchanged the beads during important ceremonies and buried them with their dead.

The Dutch began bringing large amounts of wampum to Fort Orange from downriver, where Native Americans who lived along the coast made the beads from clamshells. Indians who lived away from the coast, including some from Canada, came to Fort Orange eager to trade their furs for wampum. Soon, the Dutch themselves began using wampum as money. The beads appeared in collection plates in church, and people used them to buy land and houses.

Excavations at Fort Orange revealed that most of the bargaining between the

Dutch and the Native Americans took place just inside the fort's entryway. Large numbers of beads, likely dropped and lost during negotiations, were found there.

Woolen blankets and other fabric items were popular for trading, but these materials seldom survive in the ground. When cloth was shipped, however, lead seals (also called bale seals) covered the ropes tying the bundles. The lead bale seals survived. Impressed designs on the seals revealed the town of origin and the weave quality. One such seal found at Fort Orange contained the name CAMPEN, a town in the Netherlands. Nearby was another seal marked JVR. The house in which these seals were discovered belonged to a wealthy man named Jeremias van Rensselaer. This showed that Jeremias kept trade goods, including wool blankets, in his house.

Indian Relations

At first, the Dutch and the Native Americans cooperated to keep trade going. Then some problems developed. In 1626, the Dutch commander at Fort Orange got many of his soldiers killed while intervening in a dispute between two Native American groups. In 1655, while Governor Stuyvesant was in Delaware, Indians attacked New Amsterdam by running through the town before the Dutch were out of bed. When the Dutch pushed them off Manhattan Island, the Indians destroyed outlying farms. The Dutch did not retaliate; they paid a ransom for captives, and the conflict ended. Meanwhile, upriver halfway to Fort Orange, new problems broke out. The conflict ended in partial burning of a new Dutch town and the capture of many inhabitants. The settlers and the Indians finally signed a treaty in 1664, and the prisoners were freed.

Making Beaver Hats

Beaver hats were a fashion craze in Europe from about 1500 to 1850. Because there were many beaver in North America, the fur trade there quickly became profitable. Beaver hats were more waterproof than wool ones and held their shape better than other furs. Hat makers pulled out the guard hairs on the fur and brushed a mercury solution on the pelt to toughen the fiber. Then they dried the pelt and shaved off the fibers. When they applied heat and moisture to the pelt, the mercury was released as vapor. Because long-term exposure to mercury vapor causes damage to the nervous system, the phrase "mad as a Hatter" became a common term for someone with severe mental problems.

Hat Maker.

Wampum

Before colonizing the New World, the Dutch had encountered the use of shells as money in Africa and other places. European coins were scarce in North America. If someone dropped a coin, they looked hard for it, but archaeologists still do find a few. Native Americans used wampum to make exchanges for many years. At one time, the Dutch colonial courts set the value of wampum as money. For example, a string of eight white wampum beads discovered at Fort Orange would have been worth one stiver (a type of Dutch coin.) Purple beads were rarer and therefore worth more.

Wampum was manufactured from shells clipped into flat pieces, then rolled on a stone to make them round. A hole was drilled through the center partway from each end. A few wampum beads broken during manufacture were found in Fort Orange. In the nearby town, archaeologists found extensive evidence of wampum making, including iron drills and the stones. The Dutch settlers were making money the easy way!

Two
A Dutch Town

In the 1650s the town of Beverwyck was established north of Fort Orange. Its houses were built along a broad street that climbed up a hill. Visiting Native Americans camped at the top of the hill but strolled the streets daily and waited outside bakeshops for fresh bread and sweet rolls. They sometimes slept in Dutch houses. A local minister wrote that, while he slept in his bed one night, eight Native Americans slept on the floor at the foot of his bed.

A modern artist's painting of a Dutch ship sailing near Beverwyck, today's Albany.

Although there was little threat of attack, news of trouble elsewhere led the townspeople to build a stockade wall around the town. As Beverwyck grew, stockade lines were moved outward. Archaeologists have used these lines to trace the town's expansion over time. By 1660, Beverwyck held about a thousand people. Soon, many townspeople left to start new settlements farther south in the Hudson River Valley and farther west in the Mohawk River Valley.

A Well and a Weather Vane

This rooster weather vane once topped the Dutch Reformed Church steeple in Albany during the 1600s.

Archaeologists digging at the site of seventeenth-century Beverwyck have discovered exciting information about life there. Wooden pipes from the 1670s carried water from springs at the top of the hill to wells located in the middle of the broad central street. Dutch women must have gone to the wells several times a day to collect water and to talk. Archaeologists also found the walls of a 1656 Dutch church where two of the main streets met. Maps show that this square church had a steeple with a brass rooster weather vane. Today, the Albany Dutch Reformed Church displays this original weather vane in its church museum.

Houses, workshops, and taverns also sprawled along the river. One excavated house belonged to a local tavern owner, trader, and craftsman who glazed windows for a living. The artifacts found on the site included more than 100 pounds (45 kg) of window glass and glass waste. It appears the craftsman was very busy installing windows in local homes.

Archaeologists discovered that one street in town was paved with logs. The road surface consisted of small pine branches and logs measuring 1.5 inches (3.8 centimeters) to 8 inches (20 cm) around. Dutch artifacts such as clay tobacco pipes, yellow bricks, and glass beads were found above and among the logs. This kind of road is now called a corduroy road. Wood-paved roads like these were built well into the nineteenth century.

Archaeologists also located the town cemetery near the Dutch church. Remains of men, women, and children had been buried in wooden coffins, of which twenty-three were excavated. The coffins were lowered into burial trenches just wide enough to fit them. As was common, bodies were buried with their faces "looking" east to greet the rising sun.

A study of tooth-wear patterns on male skeletons indicated that men smoked tobacco pipes. Most held the pipes to the sides of their mouths; one held his in front. One male was especially large and had died of a staph infection in his leg. A woman's skeleton had a greenish stain at the back of the head—probably remains of a brass hair pin. Pieces of blond hair were preserved under the stain.

Discarded bones found in Beverwyck included some deer but mostly cow, sheep, chicken, and pig. The types of meat cuts showed that meat was purchased from a local butcher rather than being killed and dressed at home. This was a significant cultural change. The presence of bakeries suggests that the local inhabitants also purchased their bread rather than baking it themselves.

Another important discovery was that the Dutch adopted many Native American foods. Under the floor boards of one building lay pumpkin seeds along with butternuts and hazelnuts. These foods were new to the Dutch, but it seems they learned to enjoy them.

Tests on soil found in backyard privies (toilets) showed that the Dutch

Adventures on Ice

Between about 1300 and 1850, there was a cold period in Earth's climate history. Rivers froze during the winter, and violent storms were common. The Dutch were famous for ice-skating on their canals in the Netherlands. This tradition carried over to the New World. When the rivers froze, the colonists strapped on narrow-bladed skates to have fun and to visit nearby friends.

Another object archaeologists found was the ice-creeper. Ice-creepers were metal cleats that clamped onto people's feet for safety. Walking across frozen rivers was common, so everyone probably had a pair. It's not unusual today to see elderly people wearing these devices on their boots as they make their way across icy sidewalks and parking lots.

suffered from many parasites, a common condition in those times. Parasites cause serious health problems, which helps explain the numerous fragments of medical jars uncovered at the site.

Winter Play

The people in Fort Orange and Beverwyck were very isolated, especially in the winter when the Hudson River froze. But they stayed busy and also had fun. Numerous clay marbles and bone dice are evidence of game playing. Mouth harps continued to be popular. Narrow-bladed ice skates show that the settlers took advantage of the frozen river.

Documents tell us that the Dutch played golf in the streets. In some cases, people sued fellow colonists because of injuries that they suffered from flying golf balls! Court documents also tell of activities that were not much fun—street fights, domestic abuse, and illegal trade with Native Americans.

A Dutch Town House

Archaeologists have studied a few Dutch houses built along city streets. One such building, in the town of Wiltwyck (VILT-vik), has been excavated. In 1658, Wiltwyck was established near the Hudson River as a farming village between Fort Orange and New Amsterdam. The town grew rapidly as more and more settlers came to take advantage of the trade and the rich agricultural land surrounding the town.

The town house, now called the Matthewis Persen House, sits on a lot originally owned by a Dutch doctor who moved to Wiltwyck from Manhattan Island about 1661. He occupied a lot next to the stockade wall that had just been enlarged to accommodate the growing town. When the doctor died, an inventory revealed that he owned more than five hundred books, and his wife and children had a surprising amount of clothing and personal items. Wiltwyck may have been a frontier town, but at least some of its inhabitants were well read and well dressed.

Beads and Bodkins

Archaeologists excavated areas outside and inside the more modern house standing on the doctor's lot today. Incredibly, they found postholes from the town's upright stockade walls, as well as a burned layer from the 1663 fire. Artifacts included cannon balls, beads, wampum, clay marbles, a brass bodkin for a lady's hair, fancy drinking glasses, bricks, nails, and other building materials. The same size cannon balls and another bodkin made of silver were found at Fort Orange. The brass bodkin found at the Persen house site was much more elegant, however, despite its being made of a more basic metal. It had a sculptured hand at one end that may once have held a pearl or a precious stone. This evidence suggested, once again, that the Dutch were living much as they had in the Old World.

Three

A Dutch Farm

Although trading was the first interest of most colonists in New Netherland, the Dutch also farmed. According to historical records, the best farm of all was established north of Fort Orange along the river route that Indians took to the fort. The Dutch worked the land and stayed on the lookout for trade.

A modern artist's interpretation of a Dutch farm in New Amsterdam

After archaeologists studied Fort Orange, they wanted to look at a Dutch farm. Farm locations had been forgotten. Then, one day, archaeologists were walking in an area 4 miles (6.5 kilometers) north of the fort. They found large numbers of white clay Dutch tobacco pipes dating to the seventeenth century. Could this be a farm site?

The site was threatened by construction, so archaeologists excavated there for months and revealed that it *was* a farm site. In fact, it was the place that the records described as the "best farm."

The scientists uncovered part of a house-barn dwelling, in which people and animals shared living quarters. Under a large roof were two areas, one for people and one for the animals, with just a low wall between them. Although documents indicate that these types of houses were built in North America, no one had ever seen the remains of one. Later farms built in the Fort Orange area had separate houses and barns.

This structure was 120 feet (36.5 meters) long and 28 feet (8.5 m) wide. It was surrounded by acres of wheat and oats. The farmer's living quarters were 40 feet (12 m) long. A wood-lined cellar with wooden steps leading down from the outside was located underneath the area. In the cellar was an iron fireback with a typical Dutch patriotic scene on it. This would have been used to protect the back wall of the fireplace from flames.

The rest of the building consisted of the barn. Livestock included horses and milk cows as well as sheep and pigs. A second cellar in this area was located under a kitchen. It was similar in size to the first cellar and had its own set of wooden stairs. While the first cellar space was found clean and in good repair, the cellar under the kitchen had a 1-foot- (30.5-cm-) thick layer of garbage on the floor. Most likely people threw the trash there when they abandoned the farm.

This seventeenth-century Dutch fireback, still being used in a house in the Netherlands, is identical to one found at the Dutch farm near Albany.

Kitchen workers had access to a yellow brick courtyard that contained a cistern for collecting rainwater. In the courtyard, the Dutch could prepare food and do laundry. Farther away from the building was evidence of a palisade fence.

The archaeologists dug up artifacts including horseshoes, wagon parts, and carpenters' tools such as chisels and hammers. Smithing tools like files, hammers, and pincers, along with partially worked iron pieces, suggested the presence of a blacksmith. Most of the metal artifacts—hinges, bolts, chain links, and ice skates—probably were made right at the farm. Agricultural tools included a small hoe, a pitchfork, whetstones for sharpening tools, wedges, and a special Dutch tool called a mat hook. The settlers used mat hooks to harvest wheat, oats, and other grains.

Pewter tops that screw onto glass bottles are a common type of seventeenth-century Dutch artifact. At the farm, excavators found more than a dozen of these objects in the two cellars. Several tops were etched with codes that indicated ownership. One contained the initials AVC. It confirmed that the farm's owner was a Dutchman named Arent van Curler, who built it in 1643.

Archaeologists made an unusual discovery outside the house-barn opposite to the brick courtyard. An archaeologist uncovered a shallow pit near the front door of the house. In the center of the sandy fill were a large iron stake, two horseshoes, and an iron ring. It was a game of horseshoes!

The Dutch were not known to have played horseshoes, but the English were fond of it. The farm's owner, van Curler, had traveled to Virginia and other English colonies to sell his prized horses. Perhaps he played the game there and brought the idea back to his farm. The game might have had special appeal to him because of the horses he raised. Everyone was excited to find evidence of this new kind of Dutch behavior.

The barn site also showed evidence of trade between the settlers and the Native Americans. Excavators found Indian trade items such as lead seals that once were attached to cloth. They also found scissors, fishhooks, gun parts, and beads.

A stem from a seventeenth-century Dutch spigot, a type of faucet on barrels, found at the farm site.

Two items associated with women particularly interested the archaeologists. One was a fancy hair comb. Usually these items were made of walrus ivory, but the one discovered at the farm was made of exotic elephant ivory. The other item was a pewter top for a baby bottle. Pewter nipples like this are a rare find. This also indicated the presence of a baby in van Curler's household. Excavators discovered further evidence of van Curler's wealth: fancy gold braid from clothing, a brass book clasp for holding a thick book closed, mirror glass, and fancy shoe buckles and buttons.

Archaeologists noted big differences in food remains between the farm and the town. At the farm, the butchering and processing of meat occurred at home. Commonly eaten meat included cattle, pigs, chickens, sheep, and much more deer than in the town. The farm dwellers also ate bear, small wild animals, fish, and ducks. This frontier farmer had continued to live more off the land than had people in town.

Fragments of tin—glazed earthenware, called Delft for the town in which it was made. This plate, from a Dutch farmhouse, was decorated to imitate expensive Chinese porcelain.

Four

A Dutch Windmill and Warehouse

Although the Dutch colonists first turned their attention to the fur trade far up the North (Hudson) River, they recognized the value of the spectacular harbor at Manhattan. Between 1609 and 1614, various Dutch traders explored and mapped what is now called the New York Harbor area.

A modern artist's interpretation of a view of New Amsterdam from Governors Island in 1660.

L. F. TANTILLO 200

In 1624 Dutch settlers landed on what is now called Governors Island, located just off Manhattan Island in New York Harbor. The Indians already had cleared the small island, so it was an easy place to set up a colony. In June 1625, more colonists arrived with 103 horses and cows, as well as many pigs and sheep. Although a fort was established, it has never been found.

The Dutch used windmills at home to provide power for pumping water, sawing wood, and grinding grain. A 1639 map of Governors Island shows a windmill for sawing wood, but for a long time no one knew if the Dutch built windmills in the New World. The mapmaker could have added the windmill as a symbol of the Dutch presence in the area, not as a real structure.

An Exciting Excavation

In 1998 archaeologists working on Governors Island discovered that the Dutch did build a windmill there. This was an exciting find of a historic structure—and one so very Dutch! A circle of postholes and a circular stain were uncovered in the deepest, earliest soil layer on the island. Because the postholes were rectangular and very large, the posts that went in them were intended to support something of great weight. The circular stain and postholes suggested that the structure was about 35 feet (10.5 m) in diameter. It probably had been destroyed by fire sometime before 1650. Tests on the charcoal remains showed that the windmill was built between 1570 and 1630.

Archaeologists found part of the circular charcoal (remains of a windmill) at this site on Governors Island.

The four-bladed windmill on the map was real!

In 1626 the Dutch purchased Manhattan Island from local Native Americans for sixty Dutch guilders' worth of goods, and colonists settled on the tip of the island. Archaeologists excavating on Manhattan Island, the heart of New York City, have uncovered many remains of the Dutch colony of New Amsterdam, despite the growth of the city through time.

One of the most important finds was another typical Dutch structure—a warehouse built along the original shoreline. The Dutch went to the New World to make money from trade. They needed warehouses to store large amounts of goods before they were shipped abroad.

Another winter excavation was necessary to record the remains of this early Dutch warehouse before construction wiped out the site. The archaeologists worked beneath moveable plastic shelters weighed down

Buying Manhattan

The Dutch governor of New Amsterdam, Peter Minuit, paid the Munsee Indians sixty Dutch guilders' worth of trade goods for Manhattan Island. Although this is a tiny amount of money for such a valuable piece of real estate, the Indians probably didn't understand the concept of a land sale. To them, land belonged to everyone. Although Native Americans frequently fought over control of hunting grounds, they never believed that land belonged to them.

Above: A view of the interior of a shelter built during the warehouse excavations for protection from winter weather and occasional high winds.

Below: A cobble floor was uncovered inside the early Dutch warehouse.

BROAD STREET
CONTEXT 377
LOT 10 E ←
N30 E150
27 JAN 84

with heavy cement pods to combat brutal 55-mile-per-hour (88-kph) winds. They excavated soil layers, structures, and mysterious brick features. All dated during the Dutch colonial period that ended in 1664.

Based on their excavation of three foundation walls of the warehouse, archaeologists estimated its size at 59 feet (18 m) by 26 feet (8 m). Documents say that the warehouse was three stories high with brick walls and a tall roof. The archaeologists were able to show that the roof was covered with red tiles. The documents also report that the warehouse had a cellar and a kitchen, but neither existed at the site. Historical archaeologists often find that documents are wrong. People do not always build what they plan.

Inside the warehouse was a cobble floor, a good firm surface that kept wagons, human feet, and horses' hoofs out of the mud. Among the cobbles was a token dating to 1590. These tokens were made in Germany. The colonists used them to keep track of the number of goods being processed. The tokens are common at seventeenth-century sites.

In the backyard were two mysterious features—an oval basin and a rectangular structure made of yellow brick. Both sat just outside the rear corner of the warehouse. Most likely they were cisterns that collected rainwater for daily use.

Food for Dutch Ovens

Technicians analyzed all the artifacts from the warehouse excavation, but the food remains were especially intriguing. From 1640 to 1650, the Dutch were eating mostly cattle and some deer. By 1664, however, there was almost no deer bone. It seems the local supply already had been wiped out.

The study of plant remains showed a surprising number of European weeds already growing on Manhattan Island. Weeds had come in with shipments from Europe and quickly had begun growing in fertile ground. There were pits from peaches and cherries. By 1650 the settlers were throwing away watermelon and pumpkin seeds as their orchards and gardens began to produce. Other food remains included items found only in the New World—corn, beans, and squash. Like local Native Americans, the Dutch found corn easy to grow because it required no plowing. Pumpkins and squash could grow in the shade of the cornstalks, and beans could crawl up the stalks. The Dutch continued to use their usual cooking dishes and tableware, but they invented ways to cook these new foods.

Ways with Water—and Waste

Another fascinating find at the warehouse site was a coiled basket buried in the ground. The basket had a bottom full of holes. Inside the basket were Dutch ceramics, fish bones, nails, a musket ball, wampum beads made with iron tools, a thimble, glass beads, and sixteen marbles. At first, the archaeologists thought they had discovered a Dutch marble game. However, similar baskets had been found at other sites. They apparently were used to collect water. The holes in the bottom allowed the water to drain away slowly rather than in a big rush that would erode the soil. Occupants of the property had most likely discarded the items found in the basket.

Remains of the coiled basket found at the New York City warehouse site

Contents of the basket found at the warehouse excavation in New York City. How many items mentioned in the text do you recognize?

Diggers also uncovered barrel privies (outdoor toilets). Builders created them by inserting one bottomless wooden barrel into the top of another one. To prevent liquids from leaking out, both barrels were covered with clay and buried in the ground. Shells at the bottom of the privy vault neutralized the acid produced by human waste. A small, shedlike structure with holes for seats would have been built above the barrels. The privies were located about halfway across the backyards. This meant the warehouse occupants did not have to walk all the way to the end of the lot to use them.

Five
Other New Netherland Colonies

After the Dutch established Fort Orange on the upper Hudson River, they also built three other forts: one on the Connecticut River, one on an island off the coast of today's New Jersey, and one in today's Delaware.

Archaeological excavations at an early Dutch house site in Connecticut

Two families and six single men were sent to build Fort Good Hope on the Connecticut River. The settlement grew into Hartford, the current capital of Connecticut. Attempts to find the fort's remains have been unsuccessful. Apparently, the site was wiped out. However, excavators have found Dutch trade goods throughout southern New England and as far east as Cape Cod.

Follow the Yellow Brick

Two families and eight single men were sent to build Fort Nassau on Burlington Island in the Delaware River, in today's state of New Jersey. Following that, more Dutch colonists settled in the New Jersey area, mostly on farms along the coast. These prime locations grew into cities such as Newark, Elizabeth, Perth Amboy, and Burlington. Evidence of these Dutch settlements has been erased—or it is so deeply buried that it has not yet been found.

However, the home of a wealthy Dutch official who settled on Burlington Island has been excavated. In the 1890s an archaeologist walking there found yellow brick. Recognizing this as a seventeenth-century Dutch artifact, the archaeologist looked more closely and saw red roofing tiles and white clay pipes. After doing some reading, this early historical archaeologist, Charles Abbott, decided the site was an early Dutch trading post or tavern.

This roofing tile is from the Dutch house on Burlington Island.

A Dutch Fort in Delaware

The Dutch had problems settling in Delaware. The Swedes also claimed the land and settled nearby. In 1651 Governor Peter Stuyvesant decided to move the Dutch fort, called Fort Casimir, closer to Swedish territory. Eventually, he took over the Swedish settlement.

In the 1980s historical archaeologists drilled test holes at the site of Fort Casimir. They found a ditch moat and some stockade posts. The ditch was full of Dutch artifacts from the seventeenth century. These included a highly decorated platter with holes on the back of its base, which are evidence that it once hung on a house wall. The Dutch traders at this fort decorated their houses much as settlers had at Fort Orange. Tests run on yellow bricks showed that they had been imported. Documents revealed that these yellow bricks were from Holland and had been shipped down from Fort Orange.

Fort Casimir lies mostly in a protected area. The city of New Castle, Delaware, has left the fort site undisturbed.

Dating Clay Pipes

Early clay tobacco pipe stems had large holes. The holes grew smaller through time. Scientists have developed a formula for measuring the size of the holes in pipe stems to establish when the pipes were made. Sometimes stems and bowls also contain initials of the pipe maker or designs that identify their origin.

These fragments of red clay tobacco pipes were found at a Dutch trader's house, Burlington Island. *Courtesy of the Peabody Museum, Harvard University, Cambridge.*

Abbott dug into the sand. He found part of a wall and a section of roof covered with red tiles. Beneath them was a charred beam with burned nails. He collected pieces of bottles, a wine glass, and more than five hundred white clay pipe fragments. Abbott sent the collection to a museum, where they sat in storage until New Jersey historical archaeologists recently rediscovered them. The collection contained not only Dutch bricks, bottles, and pipes, but also more than fifty glass beads, early window glass, and some Native American artifacts. A study of the clay tobacco pipes dated them to about 1660.

One unusual find was red clay tobacco pipes. Archaeologists thought red smoking pipes were manufactured only at a much later date, but they found documentation that such pipes were made in New Jersey in the 1660s. Similar pipes have been found in Virginia and Maryland. Today archaeologists are looking more carefully at red pipes in their collections to seek evidence of a Dutch colonial pipe-making industry.

Analysis of Abbott's collection led modern historical archaeologists to conclude that the site was a house dating to the 1660s. It probably was not a Dutch trading house and certainly was not the early fort. Instead, it was the home of a Dutch governor named Alexander d'Hinoyossia, who moved his family onto the island after 1655. D'Hinoyossia had built a typical Dutch house with windows and red roofing tiles. Judging by the many glass beads at the site, he also carried on negotiations with Native Americans at his home.

Six
A Mysterious Shipwreck

In the 1650s a ship sank in the Caribbean Sea near Santo Domingo. Because the ship went down in shallow water, people were able to rescue important items like cannons and some cargo. The smaller objects in the hold were left behind.

What kind of vessel was this? Whose was it? Where was it going?

A scuba diver examines a shipwreck in the Caribbean Sea.

To answer these questions, archaeologists put on scuba gear and dove to the wreck in the early 1990s. They excavated the wooden remains and collected artifacts from the cargo hold and items associated with the lives of the crew.

The divers' study of the ship's hull suggests it was a large vessel built mostly of oak. The hull was coated with tar and cow hair and then covered with soft wood planks made of spruce to prevent it from deteriorating in salt water.

At first, the archaeologists thought they had discovered a Dutch ship. However, tests on a wooden shipboard showed it came from a tree that grew in England and was cut down in the 1640s. This proved that it was originally an English ship.

Archaeologists nicknamed this ship the Pipe Wreck because its main cargo contained thousands of white clay tobacco pipes made in the Netherlands.

Archaeologists find white clay pipes like this one.

In the 1600s tobacco smoking was an important activity, especially to the Native Americans who considered tobacco sacred. Many new settlers became addicted to the pastime. Because white clay tobacco pipes broke easily, the Dutch colonists needed a constant new supply.

Interestingly, however, this shipment contained a new kind of white clay pipe that Europeans were not known to use. It was shaped like Native American pipes. It seems that when the Dutch saw the pipe shape that Native Americans preferred, the settlers started making pipes in the same shape. Although archaeologists have found these funnel-shaped clay pipes in American Dutch and Native American sites, few have been found in Europe. The Pipe Wreck yielded the greatest number ever seen at one site. Remnants of wood and buckwheat in the hold of the ship suggested the pipes were shipped in wooden crates filled with plant material for cushioning.

The clay pipes also helped archaeologists establish a date for the shipwreck. This type of pipe was manufactured in the Netherlands after 1640.

The pipe on the left is an Edward Bird manu—factured Funnel Angle Elbow pipe, significant to the site investigation because of its rarity. The other two pipes are Bulbous Bowl pipes, popular Edward Bird designs that comprised the majority of pipes recovered on the wreck site.

What story did the rest of the artifacts tell? There were many glass trade beads, most of which were fused together by fire. Perhaps the ship had burned. The presence of beads, combs, brass bells, and thimbles strongly indicate that the vessel was supplying the fur trade. Fancy painted ceramics, brass objects associated with lighting, and fancy glassware were to be sold to wealthy colonists.

Several artifacts indicated what life was like on board the ship. Food remains were typical of the time period. There was salted meat in barrels, as well as some live animals on board. Olives and peaches supplemented the sailors' diet. There were many rats on board—and, most likely, cats. The captain or ship's doctor used a set of nested brass weights to measure small amounts of metal or medicine. Divers found navigational dividers for measuring distances on maps, as well as lead ammunition. A small ivory gaming piece suggested

PWE 1034 +
RSW Bd w/ Sprig
Molding

This is a stoneware fragment from the Pipe Wreck.

that the crew had played games to pass the time.

It was difficult to tell who owned the ship. The English had built it, but it carried many Dutch goods and seemed bound for the fur trade area of New Netherland. It is possible that the Dutch captured the ship from the English and reused it.

Historical records of one wreck might fit the Pipe Wreck story. In June 1657, a ship ran aground somewhere in the Caribbean. The date of this wreck corresponds with that assigned to the Pipe Wreck. According to the records, the ship had a Dutch crew, and sailors had removed a cargo of hides and other goods—as well as anchors and guns—before the ship had sunk.

It is impossible to know for sure what happened. However, the archaeological study of the mysterious Pipe Wreck offered new information about where and how the mysterious ship was built, what it was carrying, and something of the lives of the people on board.

Seven

What Archaeologists Found Out

The Dutch were successful in establishing colonies in North America. They did not suffer a starving time, as did some English and French settlers who established colonies before and after the Dutch. Their houses were decorated with blue hand–painted tiles. Their windows were painted with colorful designs, and their tables were set with the latest in ceramics and glassware.

A nineteenth–century woodcut depicts a Dutch family having dinner in New Amsterdam in the 1600s.

Courtyard of a House in Delft, painted by Pieter de Hooch in 1658. Many of the objects shown are identical to those excavated in America, such as yellow and red bricks, the bolt on the shutter, the wine glass, buttons, and clay tobacco pipes.

The Dutch were also quite successful in their interactions with Native Americans. They purchased land from Native peoples instead of seizing it. They set up trading posts and farms for the peaceful exchange of goods, and they welcomed Native Americans to their towns. After some serious conflicts in the Hudson Valley and New Amsterdam, however, they stockaded their living areas for increased protection from attack.

Dutch settlers learned to eat Native foods such as corn, squash, beans, and other plants. They also learned to cook deer, bear, and beaver. As best they could, they adapted to the new strange land they found. Most went to the New World to get rich from the fur trade; many stayed to farm and to establish homes.

The Dutch built houses, farms, and windmills that were surprisingly like those at home in Europe. The fronts of houses along town streets had steep, pointed roofs covered with red tiles. Wells in the street contained water carried down the hill by wooden pipes. Some of the farms had an older type of structure called a farm-barn, in which people and animals lived under the same roof. New for the Dutch, however, were the wood-lined cellars they constructed under their houses. Although houses in Holland were built on tall wooden stakes sunk into the underlying wet soil, wood-lined cellars were a new idea—and a very workable one.

Shortly after the early years, women and children arrived in the colony. They brought with them hair combs, pins, scissors, and baby bottle tops. As people grew older, they wore eyeglasses. The Dutch enjoyed themselves by ice-skating, playing golf in the street, gambling, playing tunes with mouth harps and pipe stem whistles, tossing horseshoes, reading, and trying to beat their neighbors at trade with the Indians.

"Danke" to the Dutch

Because the Dutch came early and gradually blended into the English culture that took them over, we have forgotten many of their contributions to life in North America. The Dutch values of hard work, managing money, religious tolerance, and support for the poor and handicapped have influenced American culture. Unlike the English, the Dutch had a written constitution guaranteeing people certain important rights. When the United States was established, its leaders chose to do the same. Like the Republic of United Provinces in the Netherlands, the U.S. government is a republic—a form of government in which voters elect others to represent them.

Other Dutch contributions include donuts, cookies, coleslaw, and Santa Claus. We use Dutch words like *ahoy, boss, caboose, dock, grab, landscape, measles, pickle, skate, tickle, waffle, wiggle, Yankee*, and many others. We frequent places called Brooklyn (Breuckelen), Coney Island (Konynen Eylant), Harlem (Nieuw Haarlem), Long Island (Lange Eylant), and Wall Street—named after a wall built to protect New Amsterdam. You speak Dutch almost everyday without even realizing it.

1609 Henry Hudson sails into New York Harbor and up the Hudson River to the modern-day area of Albany, New York, in his ship, the *Half Moon*.

1614 Fort Nassau is built near Albany for trade with local Native Americans.

1624 After Fort Nassau is damaged by floods, Fort Orange is built on the west bank of the Hudson River.

1625 The Dutch buy Manhattan Island from the Munsee Indians and establish a colony there.

1626 Dutch settlers land on Governors Island in New York Harbor. Forts are built in Connecticut, New Jersey, Pennsylvania, and Delaware, the area that the Dutch name New Netherland.

1629 More settlers arrive. They establish farms throughout New Netherland and trade with Native people.

1643 Arent van Curler builds "the best farm" and begins to raise crops, horses, and children north of Fort Orange.

1650 Beverwyck is established as a town west of Fort Orange.

1662 The Dutch and English go to war with each other in Europe.

1664 The English take New Netherland from the Dutch, thus uniting their English colonies into one large swath along the East Coast.

2009 Celebrations take place in New York City, along the Hudson River, Albany, and elsewhere in the old colony of New Netherland to mark the four-hundredth anniversary of the Dutch claim to land in North America.

archaeologists—Scientists who study the remains of past human life and activity.

artifacts—Human-made objects that hold historical interest.

bodkin—A slender pin of brass, gold, or silver that women wore in their hair or used to lace up clothing.

cisterns—Containers for storing rainwater.

coat of arms—A design that represents a certain family, usually a noble one.

cobble—A rounded stone used to pave streets and floors of businesses such as warehouses.

excavations—Processes of uncovering or exposing the ground through digging.

fill—Material used to fill a passage or cavity in the ground.

guard hairs—Long, coarse hairs that protect the coat of a mammal.

neutralized—To balance or lessen the effect of a chemical.

palisade—A fence made of upright or horizontal poles or stakes that is used for defending property.

parasites—Organisms that depend on other organisms, called hosts, in order to live.

pewter—A mixture of lead and tin that can easily be shaped into objects.

shorthand—An abbreviated, efficient form of writing.

staph—The short name for a type of bacteria called staphylococcus (STAF-uh-luh-KAW-kus), which can cause deadly infections.

stockade—A wall built around a town or house for protection.

strata—Distinct layers of earth that contain unique materials.

stratigraphy—The study of strata.

whetstones—Stones used to sharpen tools.

Books

David, Kevin A. *Look What Came From The Netherlands*. New York: Franklin Watts, 2002.

Fischer, Laura. *Life in New Amsterdam*. Chicago: Heinemann Library, 2003.

Lilly, Melinda. *The Dutch in New Amsterdam*. Vero Beach, FL: Rourke Publications, 2003.

Parker, Lewis K. *Dutch Colonies in the Americas*. New York: PowerKids Press, 2003.

The World Encyclopedia of Archaeology
Buffalo, NY: Firefly Books, 2007.

Websites

http://www.hudsonriver.com/history/halfmoon.htm
Information about the reproduction of Hudson's ship and links to other sites

http://www.newnetherland.org
Information about the Dutch colonies and translations of documents; links

http://nnp.org/ni/Publications/da2.html
Includes a virtual tour of the Dutch colonies

www.cobblestoneonline.net/
Various issues on archaeology and Dutch available online

Books

Bradley, James W. *Before Albany*. Albany: State University of New York Press, 2007.

Cantwell, Anne-Marie and Diana deZerega Wall. *Unearthing Gotham: The Archaeology of New York City*. New Haven. CT: Yale University Press, 2001.

DeCunzo, Lu Ann and John H. Jameson, Jr. eds. *Unlocking the Past: Celebrating Historical Archaeology in North America*. Gainesville: University Press of Florida, 2005.

Fisher, Charles L, ed. *Thirty Years of Historical Archaeology in the City of Albany, New York. People, Places, and Material Things: Historical Archaeology of Albany, New York*. Albany: The University of the State of New York, The State Education Department, 2002.

Nooter, Eric, ed. *The Birth of New York: Nieuw Amsterdam 1724-1664*. New York: The New York Historical Society and Amsterdam's Historisch Museum, 1983, pgs. 22-25.

Orser, Charles E. Jr., ed. *Encyclopedia of Historical Archaeology*. New York: Routledge, 2002.

Veit, Richard. *Digging New Jersey's Past, Historical Archaeology in the Garden State*. New Brunswick: Rutgers University Press, 2002, pg. 24-30.

Articles

Huey, Lois Miner. "The Shell Game." *dig* Magazine. Vol. 9 No. 3, March 2007, pg. 21-23.

"Under the Street." *dig* Magazine, Vol. 9, No. 8, October 2007, pg. 16-17.

"Wild Town." *dig* Magazine, Vol. 9, No. 9, November/December 2007, pg. 27-29.

Articles on the archaeology of wampum, Fort Orange, and Albany

About the Author

Lois Miner Huey is a historical archaeologist working for the State of New York. She has published many articles about history and archaeology in kids' magazines as well as a book biography of the Mohawk Indian woman, Molly Brant. She and her archaeologist husband live near Albany, New York, in an old house with four affectionate cats.

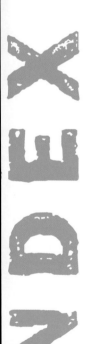

Page numbers in **boldface** are illustrations and charts.